Norse Mythology

A Guide to Norse History, Gods, and Goddesses

Jordan Parr

Table of Contents

Introduction 1

Chapter One: The World of the Norse Gods 4

Chapter Two: The Gods of the Aesir 9

Chapter Three: The Gods of the Vanir 20

Chapter Four: Norse Demigods and Others of Importance 27

Chapter Five: Monsters of Legend 33

Chapter Six: Popular Tales of the Mythology 42

Chapter Seven: Norse Mythology in Modern Media 58

Final Words 62

Introduction

In the age of Vikings, many citizens of what is now known as Norway, Denmark, and Sweden left their native soil to journey the world in search of riches. Riding the tumultuous waves of the sea, the adventurers would come to be known as raiders, pirates, traders, and settlers across the European nations and islands. This is around the time it was discovered that, to the surprise of those the Vikings bombarded, they did not belong to a Christian faith. It was not one God they swore fealty to, but instead an entire pantheon.

Between 793–1066 AD, Scandinavians continued their plunder. It is important to understand their actions through their beliefs, in which a possible sense of reason could be found. Their use of myth and storytelling to showcase their divine pantheon stems not from a place of holy magic, but instead is found in the practical world. Their numerous gods and goddesses reflect the natural world rather than a single, omnipotent presence depicted in texts. Such ideologies at the time were largely reserved for European nations, whereas the Vikings asserted and conveyed stories by word of mouth alone. Spinning the tales of those who rule the cosmos—but were still subject to the whims of fate—gave comfort in times of hardship. They found honor in the stars and legendary stories that inspired people when humanity thought they had failed. Some aspects of these stories had been lost or changed over the years, shown in the nature of preserving myths by only speaking them.

At last, inscribed in runestones came written acknowledgment of the pantheon to set the legends, quite literally, in stone. In the nineteenth century, discovered in a church in the countryside of Sweden, the Rök Rune Stone contains tales of heroes and secret pieces of Norse mythology that were forgotten over time because the denizens of Sweden had forgotten their own old language. A piece of history left behind, detailing stories of loss, great kings, and so much more that historians struggle to transcribe even today. After being moved around over many centuries, it finally found it's home in 1862 as an open display in a churchyard of Ödeshög, Sweden.

Another vital piece of these myths came in written form, a tome known only as the *Poetic Edda*. A collection of tales depicting myths and heroes alike, the manuscript was written in the time of the Vikings by numerous, unknown authors. This is perhaps one of the most integral pieces we have today to understand the old Norse mythology— and the most accurate befitting the times. It has since been translated into many different languages by several authors.

Passed through word of mouth, written in stone, and taken to page before being translated into hundreds of different languages, these mythical tales are truly held in the utmost respect to be preserved so thoroughly. They solidify the nature, the culture, and the faith of lives in centuries past. The lessons taught among the stories and the respect given to the cycle of life should be revered and cherished forever.

Chapter One: The World of the Norse Gods

The world of Germanic myth is enormous, containing not one but nine realms in which the tales take place; the first two were known as Muspelheim and Niflheim. Muspelheim is a land of only fire, a place that has little record even among historic texts aside from one mention of it being the home of Fire Giants. However, it is known to play an integral part in both the creation and demise of the world. The second realm, Niflheim, is the world of ice and cold. The complete opposite and complement to Muspelheim, it is shrouded in mist with its name literally translating to "World of Fog." (

Old Norse	Translation
Ár var alda, *þar er ekki var,* *var-a sandr né sær* *né svalar unnir;* *jörð fannsk æva* *né upphiminn,* *gap var ginnunga* *en gras hvergi.*	*That was the age when nothing was;* *There was no sand, nor sea, nor cool waves;* *No earth nor sky nor grass there,* *Only Ginnungagap.*

In the *Poetic Edda* Völuspá, stanza 3 Ginnungagap is described as a great, dark void. The translation, as seen above, has been provided by Daniel McCoy alongside the original Old Norse text.

Between Niflheim and Muspelheim rested a great abyss, a chasm known only as Ginnungagap. Something unknown caused the two realms to meet in the center, where the ice and fire created a giant, who was originally referred to as a *jötunn* in Nordic languages but was named Ymir, and the icy cow Audhumla. Ymir, his body composed of ice and fire, is considered in the old tongue to be a hermaphrodite. The use of the word hermaphrodite is used with Ymir to describe "one who gives birth" despite being frequently referred to as male. This term is evidently used several times in different Nordic legends to describe similar situations in which people or monsters spring forth from someone known to be male in legends. It is notable, however, that the term historically was also used to describe androgyny, being effeminate, or even twins. It may even refer to the fact that he was born of fire and ice, two complete opposites thought to be incapable of harmony. Rarely was it ever used to describe someone with two different sets of sexual organs in the age of Vikings. While the giant Ymir slept, many children sprang forth from several different parts of his body.

From his foot sprang forth a son, then the heat of Muspelheim caused a man and a woman to be born from the sweat of his armpits—all of them giants. His fertile sweat then bore the giant of fire, Surtr. To cool his great heat, Ymir woke to drink the milk of the ice cow, Audhumla, while it licked salt off a stone. From the stone where Audhumla licked, another man slowly emerged who would come to be known as Buri, who then copulated with the giant woman of Ymir's sweat, known as Bestla, to give birth to Bor. Bor would become the father of three gods: Vili, Ve, and Odin.

Ymir, being a giant to eclipse all other giants, was a formidable opponent to his grandsons. Chaos personified, Odin and his brothers saw Ymir as a threat to their continued livelihood, wishing for a world without chaos that they could freely rule. They plotted, and ultimately succeeded, to murder Ymir. From his enormous body, the cosmos finally could be crafted to take form.

Old Norse	Translation
Ór Ymis holdi *var jörð of sköpuð,* *en ór sveita sær,* *björg ór beinum,* *baðmr ór hári,* *en ór hausi himinn.* *En ór hans brám* *gerðu blíð regin* *Miðgarð manna sonum,* *en ór hans heila* *váru þau in harðmóðgu* *ský öll of sköpuð.*	*From Ymir's flesh* *the earth was created,* *And from his sweat [or blood]* *the sea,* *Mountains from bone,* *Trees from hair,* *And from his skull the sky.* *And from his eyebrows* *the blithe gods made* *Midgard,* *home of the sons of men* *And from his brains* *They sculpted the grim clouds.*

In the *Poetic Edda* Grímnismál, stanzas 40–1 describe the macabre sculpting of Midgard from the corpse of Ymir. Translation has been provided by Daniel McCoy, which may be seen above alongside the original Old Norse text.

Odin, Vili, and Ve wasted no time filling the Ginnungagap with the ornaments of the corpse of Ymir. Before long, the void was filled with the world of Midgard. As the blood of chaos filled Midgard, all but two giants drowned. Soon thereafter, these two giants would reclaim their same numbers as before and replenish the population of the jötunn. The three brothers, all contributing equally, created Ash and Elm, the first man and woman to walk Middle-earth. After the creation of Midgard, the other seven worlds of the nine would soon become realized.

The next realm to be created became known as Asgard, which would become home to gods of the Aesir. These gods represented order, war, and structure with some of the more well-known gods in the pantheon. Beside Asgard came Vanaheim, the realm of the Vanir gods. The Vanir, in contrast to the Aesir, took focus on nature and fertility. To connect the realms, Odin created the Bifrost Bridge, which would become known to the humans he created as the Rainbow Bridge. This bridge would connect the rest of the realms that came soon after. Jotunheim, where the giants came to live after being banished from Midgard. Alfheim, home to elves who were considered to be nearly as powerful, and as ethereal, as demigods. Svartalfheim, the world of the dwarves that first came to be after Midgard was formed. Then finally, Hel, the world of the dead, likened to the underworld that becomes home to mortal spirits after they have passed on. Occasionally, it is referred to also—perhaps to fit the motif of the other worlds—as Helheim.

The nine worlds, Midgard, Asgard, Vanaheim, Jotunheim, Niflheim, Muspelheim, Alfheim, Svatalfheim, and Hel are all connected by the great, cosmic tree known as Yggdrasil. Aside from Midgard, the other eight worlds are considered to be invisible to the eyes of humans, but despite this they are known to occasionally manifest into the material world. Notably, nine is a holy number in the Germanic tribes that this mythology hails from. It is a repeated pattern in the stories that would follow from the Allfather, Odin, and his many sons, daughters, adversaries, and allies.

Chapter Two: The Gods of the Aesir

Odin, The All-Father

After creating the worlds of Midgard and Asgard with his two brothers, Odin began referring to himself as the "All-Father" because he was responsible for the creation of the world of mortals, and subsequently many of his children that would become various gods of the material world. He is often portrayed throughout "The Poetic Edda" to not care about matters of kinship, instead favoring the practical elements of life. In the pursuit of power, honor, and wisdom, he is considerably relentless, self-sacrificing, boastful, war-hungry, and stubborn. He has also been known to claim fallen warriors for his prestigious Valhalla, where the dead may be tended to as though they were kings in celebration of their honor in life. To the delight of Vikings, the qualities Odin portrayed were seen as extremely masculine and often inspired many to fight in his name during their plunders. Even if it was only in the smallest hope that the All-Fathers' Valkyries will arrive upon their deathbed to claim them.

Some odd facts do contradict his masculine nature. He is also known to be a refined poet; many say he spoke only in poems. In addition, he practiced a type of magic known as *Seidr*. This magic was thought of in mythology to primarily be a feminine practice and was even considered shameful in the male-gender roles of the society he created. Considering his focus was mostly on the art of necromancy, which is raising the dead to fight for him, and clairvoyance, in which he would try to tell the future for the sake of his kingdom, it certainly didn't affect the level of respect Odin received from his worshippers.

Odin, despite calling himself the All-Father, had only ever contributed to one third of the creation of mortal humans. The other two contributors were his brothers, Vili and Ve, who were given parts of Asgard to rule before they unceremoniously disappeared into obscurity. In Old High German, the name Odin translates to "master of ecstasy."

Frigg, Wife of Odin

Frigg, sometimes also known as Frigga, is wife to the All-Father and mother to the god of beauty, Baldur. Unfortunately, little is written about the goddess and her role in Asgard. She was once considered to be one and the same goddess as the Vanir Freya, and it wasn't until late into the historical record that she became her own, distinct deity. Despite this, there is still much debate if Frigg and Freya are indeed *not* the same person, as translations of old tomes give conflicting evidence of either possibility. It may be that Freya, a name which means "lady," was seen as too promiscuous to share the same seat as the wife Frigg, whose name means "beloved."

Frigg is depicted as a wielder of Nordic magic, *Seidr*, and often uses her powers of clairvoyance to aid Odin in his attempts to change the nature of fate. As Odin is often away from Asgard, Frigg has been accused on more than one occasion of adultery against her husband, as she had allegedly slept with a slave while he was away on duty. Furthermore, it is also said that Odin's brothers, Vili and Ve, had also slept with Frigg. This may be a possible reason why the two *mysteriously* disappear from the tales of the pantheon.

Thor of Thunder

Thor, the warrior god of thunder, with a name that literally means thunder, may be one of the most well-known gods in the entire pantheon, next to Odin and Loki. With his trusted hammer Mjöllnir and a chariot drawn by goats, Thor protected all of Asgard from the attacks of giants who wished to enact their revenge upon Odin for dismantling their former way of life. Aside from the Giants, Thor's nemesis may indeed be Jörmungandr, the giant serpent whose massive body circles around Midgard. While the two clash several times over the course of several different stories, it is not until Ragnarok, the battle for the end of the world, when they face in their final showdown. Thor's strength, as a son of Odin and the giantess Jord, is unmatched. Although he is often seen to be an undeniably valiant and courageous figure in mythology, he has several talents that are often untold in modern retellings of his prowess.

For example, while Mjöllnir is known to be able to destroy and defend, Thor has also used the same hammer to heal, create, and even give blessings. The name of Thor was called on to bless weddings, give comfort in times of hardship, bless land before planting crops or buildings, and even used to promote fertility. While his name specifically alludes to thunder, he is seen as a sky god in his entirety, meaning he controls all weather and subsequently affects farmer's crops and trade. His connection to the harvest undoubtedly plays a role with his wife, Sif, who is considered to be an earth goddess.

Odin and Thor, being polar opposites in their values and beliefs, often butt heads over even minor of disagreements. Despite this, Thor is loyal to Asgard and several times more popular among worshippers of the Old Norse deities. Once Christianity came to Scandinavia, and the invading forces refused to respect their traditions, it was not Odin that believers called upon for protection, but the might of Thor that their prayers extended to the heavens for. To hide their true beliefs from Christians, worshippers wore small, miniature pendants of Thor's iconic hammer on necklaces as signals to one another that they believed in the pantheon. This was in silent protest to the crosses Christians wore, effectively making Thor himself the very symbol of Old Nordic religion.

Sif of the Bountiful Harvest

Sif is the beautiful earth goddess of the Aesir and is often associated with the harvest in addition to her husband Thor. The union of an earth goddess and a sky god would produce the most bountiful collection a farmer could procure. Not much is written of Sif, due to her being widely overshadowed by her partner. She is mentioned in passing within the most archaic writings, which makes her a once widely recognized and important goddess. While her contributions to politics did not make her especially notable in the *Poetic Edda,* her symbolic ones mattered greatly to the people of Scandinavia, which garnered respect from those who worshipped her.

Thor is in fact her second husband, her first was a giant by the name of Orvandil, with whom she had a son named Ullr. Ullr would become the obscure god of winter—and skiing. With Thor, Sif gave birth to a daughter whose name, Thrúd, means strength. Though she shares a name with a Valkyrie that will survive Ragnarok, it is unclear if they are the same person. She is the goddess of power, trees, flowers, and grass. Which means, in essence, Sif is the mother of spring and winter.

A notable feature of the Goddess Sif is her beautiful and long golden hair, which later became the victim of a prank by Loki, who had cut her hair off completely only to quickly find a way to replace her hair in terror of Thor's reaction. She is adored and loved by Thor, who values her intelligence and beauty. Her name means "relation to marriage."

Loki the Master of Chaos

Of equal notoriety to Thor but thrice known in infamy, Loki the Trickster God is son of the Giant Farbauti and the unknown entity Laufey or Nal, who goes by both names. His mother may have been a giantess or goddess, but there appears to be no evidence to support the claim of either. This makes Loki something of an enigma, a factor that plays a role in his mannerisms juxtaposed to the other gods and goddesses of the pantheon. Being the offspring of an unknown entity and a giant, it only seems natural that he seeks to end Odin's reign with the coming of Ragnarok and bring back the chaos that existed before the formation of the realms. Even his name, which has been translated as "to tangle or knot" foreshadows that he is the tangle in the thread of fate that will forever upend the Norse gods.

However, not all of Loki's exploits are necessarily so dark. Tales of him playing pranks on his unsuspecting cohorts are meant to teach lessons to those who listen, not unlike bedtime stories for children. Though, arguably more mature content is usually featured in his stories, and so they can be used for a wider audience. The powers of the trickster god echo his mastery of some chaotic magic, crafting illusions and transforming into any shape he chooses at any given time. Though this power would be magnificent on its own, it is shared by an impressive intellect and cunning that is matched only by his sense of ambition. He has a knack for exploiting weaknesses, insecurities, and fooling people into either harming themselves or others. Typically seen as a coward, the other gods consider him an obstacle rather than one of their own. Their feelings are not unfounded, as in one tale he causes the death of beauty, the god Baldur. It is perhaps no wonder that he is an integral key to the events that would shape Ragnarok.

Loki is generally referred to as male, but he changes forms several times over the course of the religion's history, including a shift in gender. Even both fathering *and* mothering children, which range from minor gods to monsters that ultimately play a role in the cause of Ragnarok. With the giantess Angrboda, Loki's offspring include the queen of the Underworld, Hel, the serpent who would kill Thor, Jörmungandr, and Fenrir, the wolf who becomes nemesis to Odin himself. These children are destined to harm and kill many Asgardians who may have considered him kin, and he in turn appears to scorn the rules and order of Asgard.

By a proper Asgardian mate, his wife Sigyn, Loki has two sons named Nari and Váli who would eventually meet a tragic fate by the hands of the Aesir Gods themselves. Sigyn (her name meaning "Friend of Victory,") was apparently an extremely dutiful and loyal wife to Loki, staying by his side even as he faced extreme punishment for his actions by his kinsmen.

Tyr of War

Tyr is the god of war in Norse mythology, but his other duties also make him a god of law and justice. He is considered to be the bravest warrior of the Aesir and lost a hand—or an entire arm, depending on the translation—to the great wolf, Loki's son Fenrir. Due to this attribute, he is referred to as the "One-handed God."

There is some debate over the nature of Tyr's lineage, with some scholars debating if he is a son of Odin or a son of a giant named Hymir. The most concrete evidence of his lineage is that he has a grandmother with nine hundred heads. Regardless of whoever sired the god of war, he was treated as an equal among his siblings and would eventually become integral to the battle of Ragnarok.

He is a major enough god to even be recognized by the Romans, who even invoke him under the name *Mars*. Tyr's Nordic name, however, translates to "god" when taken from the Proto-Germanic word *tiwaz*.

Vidar the Silent Vengeance

Vidar is a very mysterious individual throughout the course of Norse mythology. He says very little and is often only mentioned in passing. Most of his role is considered only vital to the events that unfold during Ragnarok, elsewhere there is not much said of him. He has been called in some places *the silent god*, an extremely unusual label for a son of Odin and a giantess, Gríðr.

His might is nothing to sneeze at. Though he is shy and ultimately withdrawn from the drama the other gods have between each other, his strength is second only to his brother, Thor. As such, after Odin was slain by the wolf Fenrir during Ragnarok, Vidar attacked his father's murderer, slicing his throat and jaw to ribbons. The monster was felled forever, marking Vidar's revenge for his father's death.

Who is this fearsome warrior who had been close enough to Odin to go into a rampage after his death, yet so aloof that he stays away from the day-to-day lives of his kin? To be so peaceful yet fly into such a formidable rage upon a moment's notice? To become so important in the events at the end of days that he stops the killer of the All-Father himself, then disappears into obscurity in all other forms of written history in Norse mythology? It is unlikely archeologists will uncover any further stories of Vidar in the near future, if at all. This untitled, unknown god who helped put a stop to the end of the world is, unfortunately, the unsung hero of the gods themselves. His name may provide some clues, however. The name Vidar' translates to "the Wide-Ruling One," a meaning that certainly arouses some amount of curiosity as to his role.

Heimdall the Guardian

At the beginning of the Bifrost Bridge is a fortress called Himinbjörg, or the Sky Cliffs. This is where the guardian of Asgard, Heimdell, born of Odin and nine different mothers, stands vigilant. With eyes that can see hundreds of miles, hearing so acute he can hear the grain growing in the fields, and his iconic horn, Gjallarhorn, which he blows to signal an alarm when enemies are near, he is a well-respected member of the pantheon. Historians are unsure the meaning of his name, but some think it to mean "one who illuminates the world."

According to the *Poetic Edda*, he would often visit mortal women who would bear his children, creating the three races of man.

He is well-humored enough to suggest Thor disguise himself as a bride to get his beloved hammer back when it is stolen, a tale which will be explained in further detail later. In Ragnarok, it is Heimdall who would end up striking down Loki in the end, who in turn is slain at the same time. The two have always considered themselves to be enemies.

Hodr the Blind

Hodr, sometimes called Hod, is the blind god of winter and darkness. He only appears in one tale, in which he is tricked by Loki into murdering his twin brother, Baldur, by using the only item in the world known to be his weakness. His blindness made him unaware as Loki handed him a spear of mistletoe, which he then launched at Baldur in jest. Baldur died instantly, falling on the spot. Despite this being an accident, Hodr was murdered in revenge by an obscure god, another son of Odin named Vali. This story has a few different iterations, but the murder of Baldur at his hands remains consistent.

Baldur of Beauty

Luminous, charming, handsome, and cheerful, Baldur is the god of joy, summer, and light. Every single God, aside from the jealous Loki, adored Baldur. A son of Odin, Baldur confides in his mother, Frigg, when he has dreams foretelling of his death. Frigg, concerned for her beloved son, uses her power as a goddess to speak to all materials. She asks them to not hurt her son, and the loyal inanimate objects and animals alike obey her wish. Loki later inquires about this, and she admits to him that she did forget to ask one material; mistletoe.

However, Frigg quickly writes it off as being unimportant, as mistletoe to her is but a harmless plant.

Baldur, inspired by his new sense of invincibility, allows his kinsmen to throw their weapons at him in jest. All the god's jovially throw all they can at Baldur, only to see that Frigg's plan to leave her son unharmed worked as intended. That is, of course, until his brother, Hodr, had his turn to play Baldur's game. After this, Loki spitefully goes on to obstruct the possibility of Baldur's resurrection by means of deceit and transformation.

Forseti the Meditative

In a house made of gold and silver named Glitnir, Forseti—his name meaning "president" in modern Icelandic—acts as judge for the Aesir gods' often unruly disputes. Little is known about Forseti, other than his rule as keeper of the peace among his cohorts, and that he is considered, like Heimdall, to be a god of justice. He enjoys his time not untangling the squabbles of others in meditation. Some scholars speculate the possibility that he is the son of Baldur, but there is little evidence to give this claim any repute.

Chapter Three: The Gods of the Vanir

"Then all the powers went to the judgment seats
the very holy gods, and discussed this:
whether the Aesir should pay a fine,
or all the gods should have tribute.
That was yet the battle of armies, the first one in the world.
Odin let fly and shot into the army,
The shield wall of the fortress of the Aesir was broken,
The battle-wise Vanir knew how to tread the field."

—Snorri Sturluson, Völuspá Stanzas 23–4
Translated by John Lindow

At the beginning of time—that is, after Odin formed Midgard—another set of Gods became known. Little is written of those that made their home in Vanaheim, though they would be named Vanir to separate themselves in the written history of Norse mythology. The meaning of the name '*Vanir*' is unknown, but the gods that are represented from Vanaheim are generally considered to be more in touch with nature. If Asgard represents order, then Vanaheim represents a sort of natural chaos, though none so much as the world that existed with the Ginnungagap and Ymir.

Most of the Vanir gods rule over some order of the natural world, such as the sea or forests. Even this distinction is not necessarily accurate, as the thunder that the Aesir Thor rules over, is natural. If you look closer, however, and see that Frigg, his mother, and the Vanir goddess Freya may have been the same person, we can conclude his inheritance of ruling this chaotic power even in the world of order that the All-Father builds.

With this natural-world chaos standing in the world untamed, Odin quickly found himself in conflict with it. This spurred the Aesir-Vanir war, which eventually would end in truce on both sides. In time, the Aesir and the Vanir merged, with some members becoming integral to the Aesir, like Frigg/Freya. Still, it is important to understand the distinction of the two, and who they were before the two converged.

Vanaheim

Vanaheim is the world in which the Vanir reside, and one of the nine worlds connected by the great tree, Yggdrasil. The Vanir represent the chaos of the natural world and are often associated with fertility. Though there are no concrete descriptions of what this world was like, due to the connection of chaos or the wild, scholars often assume that this area must be like a grand, untamed forest. A complete contrast to the orderly, high structures of Asgard.

Freyr the Lustful

Freyr—his name meaning Lord, and sometimes called Frey—is the fertility god of rain and sunshine and is considered to be the leader of the Vanir. He would eventually take a seat as an honorary member of the Aesir, with many legends even describe him as working directly beside Thor. This is not hard to imagine. Thor's wife, Sif, being a harvest goddess often meant the three would work together to produce the best harvest possible among those dwelling in Midgard. It could even be ventured, academically speaking, to guess that the three may have been good friends after the Aesir-Vanir war. Despite being welcome among the Aesir and the Vanir, Freyr prefers to live in the world of the elves, Alfheim.

Freyr's role in the livelihood of every soul in Midgard was at the mercy of his benevolence. Sexual and ecological fertility, bountiful harvests as mentioned before, wealth, and lasting peace were only a few of the gifts Freyr's presence was known to bestow upon his worshippers. An appearance of Freyr among men, drawn in on his chariot pulled by his golden boar Gullinborsti, often resulted in feuds being put to rest and replaced by celebration and joy that often came in the form of festivals. Sacrifices to the god were not unheard of, truly marking how well-revered Freyr was, despite his origins in the Vanir.

Freyr has been depicted in statue form—under the guise of another name and worshipped beside Thor—as having an enormous phallus and being a sexual partner of several different figures in Norse mythology. Suitably, he was the lover of many of the goddesses, giantesses, and even his sister Freya. One such story claims that he stayed the night with a priestess of Frey, and her following pregnancy is attributed to be an example of his powers of fertility.

He is, in addition to being a bountiful god of fertility, a great warrior who would participate in, and ultimately fall during, Ragnarok. Freyr had given to his friend a sword that could slay giants, which he would later come to regret during battle. He was able to hold his own, felling the giant Beli with an antler, only to be killed after being tired out by another giant, Surt, in the midst of Ragnarok.

Njord of the Sea

John Lindow translates a description of this god from the *Poetic Edda*, originally written by Snorri Sturluson.

> *"He governs the movement of the winds and controls the sea and flame; it is to him you should pray for voyages and fishing. He is so rich and prosperous that he can grant prosperity of land or property to those who pray to him."*

Njord, meaning of the name unknown, is often considered part of the Vanir, though after the war, he would often convene in Asgard as an honorary member of the Aesir. His name was one invoked frequently by the Vikings, who wished their plunders to be plentiful and their voyages swift. Many often desired to be "as rich as Njord."

Once, when appearing in Asgard during a council meeting, the giantess Skadi appeared and demanded some form of restitution for her father, who was murdered by one of the Aesir. In settlement, it was agreed upon that she may choose any of the gods present to be her husband. Mistaking him for Baldur the Beautiful—which speaks volumes about Njord's appearance—Skadi selects him to be her husband.

As the tale goes, it was a miserable affair. Skadi hated the realm that belonged to Njord, and he despised the frigid mountains where she lived. The marriage did not last long, and the two eventually went their separate ways. He would go on to father the Vanir god and goddess, Freyr and Freya respectively, with a sister who is unnamed.

Freya, the Displaced Goddess

Freya, or sometimes Freyja, is widely debated to be one and the same as Frigg, Odin's wife. Indeed, once the Aesir-Vanir war is over, it is Njord, Freyr, and Freya who appear among the Aesir most frequently, with the distinction of Frigg and Freya being debated by several scholars over time.

Before she may have become known to be Frigg, she was a free-spirited goddess who adored celebrations, fine material possessions, love, beauty, and fertility. She is considered to be the goddess of love, sex, and femininity. Her main mode of transportation is a chariot drawn by cats, and her control of the wild magic, *Seidr*, is unmatched by any of her family and associates—a trait that would be later exploited by Odin.

Freya's free-spirited nature among the Aesir was perfect for Loki's ploy to accuse her of sleeping with many of the gods, elves, and her own brother—though the last part is accurate, among the Vanir incest is evidently common and certainly not frowned upon. She is, however, very intelligent and found ways to ensure that Loki's words wouldn't smother her reputation with Odin. Though in some forms of modern media, her relationship with the All-Father is often shown to be rocky. There are a few tales detailing the fact that she would weep golden tears each time he left her side, indicating she at least cared for the order-loving, Asgardian god. That is, if she is indeed Frigg. By comparing the similar stories of the two, many conclude that Frigg and Freya must be one and the same.

Freya, or Frigg, has two daughters by Odin who are not often spoken of, Gersemi and Hnoss.

Gullveig the Impervious

A strange goddess who is mostly mentioned during the Aesir-Vanir war itself, Gullveig also goes by the name Heid and is said to have possibly instigated the war itself by entering Odin's Hall in Asgard and performing the first known instance of *Seidr*. Among the Aesir, she is considered a witch and is attempted to be burned, but survives. Her second name, Heid, is later attributed to witches that exist in other Norse legends. There is some speculation that she may also be another version of Freya/Frigg due to the nature of her name roughly translating to "golden drink", as Freya or Frigg is said to have wept golden tears and is the owner of some amount of material wealth.

Considering some scholars also consider her to be Freya/Frigg, the likely turn of events—though strange—may be that her birth name is Freya, her warrior name is Gullveig, and her matronly name among the Aesir is Frigg. This theory is only based on speculation.

Old Norse	Translation
Þat man hon folkvíg fyrst í heimi, er Gullveigu geirum studdu ok í höll Hárs hana brenndu, þrisvar brenndu, þrisvar borna, oft, ósjaldan, þó hon enn lifir.	She remembers the war of peoples first in the world, When Gullveig with spears they studded And in Har's hall burned her; Thrice burned, thrice born, Often, unseldom, though she yet lives.

She was attacked, but could not be killed, according to this statement from one of the *Poetic Edda* poems, Völuspá stanza 21, as translated by Lindow.

Chapter Four: Norse Demigods and Others of Importance

Bragi of Eloquence

A remarkable character that is noted among the Aesir Gods, Bragi Boddason (Bragi meaning "Poet"), was once a living, breathing human being of Midgard. His poetry and songs were so moving that, upon his death, he was employed by Odin in Valhalla where he would be a bard for the greatest warriors of the dead. The legends eventually ascend him from court bard to becoming the god of poetry, and he is married to Idun, who would have provided him the possibility of becoming a god in the first place. The god of poetry is described as having runes carved on his tongue, perhaps to further enhance his craft. Interestingly, there is no evidence of him being worshipped as a god.

Idun of Youth

Half dwarf, Idun is the beautiful goddess of spring and immortality who maintains, guards, and supplies the fruit of immortality—which she works tirelessly to harvest—to the gods. The gods, despite their status, are not immune to the effects of time. Idun's extremely important role among the Aesir is to maintain her orchard so that the Aesir may eat her crops and keep their youthful beauty. Her husband, Bragi, is so infatuated with her that if she leaves him at all, he is unable to compose any music or write poetry in the absence of his muse.

Kvasir the Keeper of Knowledge

Kvasir is another obscure figure among the myths. Born from the treaty of peace that came at the end of the Aesir-Vanir war, the gods from both sides of the warring factions spat into a vessel as a symbol of their agreement to end the war. From this spit, a god or man was formed; this was Kvasir. His name means "fermented berry-juice" and is connected to the Nordic making of mead or alcohol at the time—the Norwegian word for liquors being *kvase*. Due to the nature of his birth, Kvasir was born very wise and is considered to be among the most intelligent of both the Aesir and the Vanir. He would travel Midgard teaching the common folk all he was able to. In the legend called the "Mead of Poetry," Kvasir's blood is drawn by dwarves who are hosting him for the night, and then that blood ferments into the mead the legend is named after.

Hel of the Underworld

Hel is the goddess daughter of Loki and her giantess mother, Angrboda. Her name matches the realm that she was given by Odin in exchange for her lodging the spirits of those who died of sickness or old age. The world she rules, Helheim, is described as something of a frozen wasteland, while the hall she resides in, a palace of ice, is named Eliudnir. She is described as having a body that is half charcoal black and half flesh-toned, infamous for her constantly grim expression as she oversees her realm. In the poems and tales that she is featured in, she is harsh toward any guests in her realm. In true macabre fashion, the ornaments and tools of her home are named after various plagues of men. Most notable of which is her dish, Hungr (hunger), and her knife Sultr (famine).

Mimir the Wise

Mimir's presence throughout the *Poetic Edda* is consistent, but his lineage is uncertain, with that source claiming he is either an Aesir God or a giant. The name Mimir means "the Rememberer" and is fitting for one as wise as him. Mimir was a counselor to the Aesir gods who, during the Aesir-Vanir war, were taken by the Vanir as hostage with his comrade Hoenir. The Vanir, seeing that Hoenir was a bumbling fool who wouldn't dare act without Mimir's suggestion, saw Mimir as a threat to the war's purpose for his wisdom. Mimir is then beheaded by an unknown member of the Vanir, and the head was sent back to Odin as a message.

Odin quickly preserves Mimir's head and reanimates it so he may still take counsel with him. Without a body, the talking head of Mimir seldom leaves Odin's side, and his wisdom is often sought-after by the All-Father when in need of advice. The legends and sources of mythology consider these two to be friends.

Hoenir the Feeble

Hoenir is a tall, beautiful god among the Aesir that is given no title nor any jurisdiction, but instead serves as Odin's right hand in many tales of Odin's travels with Loki. He is even said to be present at the creation of the first of man and woman. As he is not credited outright, it can be assumed he only aided Odin with his portion of creation along with Vili and Ve.

During his service to Odin, he was taken by the Vanir as a hostage. The Vanir, so taken with Hoenir's beauty, immediately made him their chieftain. However, Hoenir's incompetence came to light when he could not make any decisions at all unless Mimir was present. In the mythology, he appears only to be useful as a companion and nothing else.

The Norns

The Norns—pronounced "norm" with an M rather than an N from Old Norse—are female figures of Norse Mythology that are said to control the fate of all the nine worlds. Comparing a few scholarly notes, the *Poetic Edda* cites there being three main Norns named Urd, Verdandi, and Skuld that live in the trunk of Yggdrasil. While these three shape the fate of the world, other Norns exist that visit each person, elf, and dwarf upon their birth to determine the fate of each life they touch. Depending on how noble or wicked the Norn is, they are to blame for how grand or miserable an individual's life can become.

Valkyries

As the "choosers of the slain," Valkyries work hand in hand with the Norns in deciding the fate of those who die in battle. It is a misconception that these fearsome female warriors only take away the souls of those that die fighting; instead, they work by weaving macabre looms with thread made of intestines, severed heads for weights, and swords and arrows for beaters. They are known to use malicious magic to ensure they get their way when things look undesirable on the battlefield. They are the weavers of fate for those they select to join Valhalla, bloodthirsty warriors, and in several tales the lovers of mortal men.

Curiously, when they aren't choosing souls to claim for their own or taking mortal lovers, the *Poetic Edda* details how they are waitresses in the dining halls of Valhalla, tending to food and drinkware while keeping company with those that are within.

Elves

Residing in Alfheim and governed by the God Freyr, Elves and those of the Vanir are very closely related in terms of their connections with nature. The magic they practice is not dissimilar to that of Seidr, which the Vanir have mastery over, being able to create and heal diseases or manipulate matters of nature and fertility. Like Gods, Elves were worshipped in Scandinavia during the Viking Age. This may be because they are described as being very ethereal and extremely beautiful as beings made of light. At one point, the translators of the *Poetic Edda* believed there to be a distinct faction of two different kinds of elves, light and dark. However, due to the nature of the Old Norse term svartalfar, and the dwarven realm, Svartálfaheimr, it has since been concluded that this is simply another term used to refer to the dwarves.

Dwarves

In the world of Norse Mythology, dwarves were the very literal pillars of Midgard. After the defeat of Ymir, four dwarves whose translated names mean North, South, East, and West took the corners of the sky (Ymir's skull) and held it above the land. They are described as having pitch-black skin, some resembling human corpses, and work in underground tunnels smithing some incredible tools. One of their creations being Thor's own hammer, Mjölnir. Despite how they are currently portrayed in modern media, there is no evidence in the writings of the *Poetic Edda* to describe them as being small, and there is no actual translation as to what the word "dwarf" means.

Chapter Five: Monsters of Legend

Jötunn, the Giants

The main source of the battles with gods, the Jotunheim-dwelling titans often fiercely waged war against Odin. Desperately, they would seek to return the world to the state that Ymir lived in, a realm of chaos and the Ginnungagap, which they all saw as home. Two very different types of giants make up a very distinct set of factions, one being the mountain giants and the other the frost giants.

At the beginning of time, when Ymir's sweat was filling the void with many offspring, the giants would do nothing but devour them. Being as massive as they are, the amount of food needed to satiate their hunger was immense, which fed into Odin's disgust. The result of him and his brothers defeating Ymir was him taking over the realm for himself. But before the All-Father could destroy the last of the jötunn, the remaining few survivors from the bastardization of Ymir's corpse managed to escape. They made a home for themselves in the new land, Jotunheim. From there, the relationship between the gods of the Aesir and the jötunn of Jotunheim was forever tense. Though some of the gods do take lovers among the giants and vice-versa, it is over time that the hatred and fear of each other has built. This culminated in Ragnarok, the great reset of power when those representing order, in this case the gods, and those representing chaos, in this case the jötunn, wage war.

Though it would be easy to write off the giants as being creatures of pure evil considering their gluttonous beginnings and what they represent, the ideology of what is good and evil is a fairly Christian concept. Instead, the giants are representative of wild and untamed magic, a natural world that has yet to be claimed by those who wish to establish their settlements using machinery or modern implementations that would harm the world as it is. Likewise, the gods are imperfect in Norse mythology and behave very humanly. The feuds, battles, and arguments all come together to form what is the eclipse during the era of Ragnarok. The gods struck down many giants, and many giants sought only to harm the gods. On the other hand, many were lovers to the gods, with Thor himself being three-quarters giant. It is no surprise that in the end many of those in the battle of Ragnarok met their demise, and the survivors were left to pick up the pieces.

Jörmungandr, the World Serpent

His name literally translates into "the Midgard Worm," Jörmungandr was born to the god Loki and the giantess Angrboda, along with his siblings Hel and Fenrir. Referred to in the *Poetic Edda* as the Midgard-Serpent, Jörmungandr was born a size small enough to fit in the palm of a human hand. However, once Odin laid eyes upon the tiny snake, he was so alarmed by the potential danger it could cause that he threw it into the sea. There, the serpent learned to survive, growing so massive that he would eventually come to circle all of Midgard, with his massive body resting in the sea.

Many scholars describe the snake as being horrible, venom-spitting, and vicious. Despite this, there are only three stories in which Jörmungandr is prominently featured, none of which suggest him to be a malevolent presence. The first is when Thor, challenged to lift Jörmungandr's tail that was disguised with an illusion to appear as a housecat, was able to only lift the cat's paw and frighten the giants who witnessed it. In the same story where Thor is convinced the serpent is a cat, he is also challenged to duel an old lady. He fails humorously, and it turns out the elderly woman is none other than "Old Age" herself, and no one can defeat old age.

In the second story, Thor accidentally wrangled in Jörmungandr while fishing using an ox-head as bait. The serpent, seeing who had him, was terrified and fought, spewing his venom at Thor and trying his hardest to avoid being caught. Thor nearly killed him with his hammer, but the giant accompanying him, frightened by Jörmungandr's presence, cut the line with a knife. Jörmungandr sank back into the sea, relieved to live another day.

The final story features the serpent in Ragnarok, when Thor and he meet once again. This time, they are to battle until death. Thor strikes down Jörmungandr after a long battle, but having been bitten, the venom took hold of his life after taking only nine steps away from the corpse. A few sources cite these two as being mortal enemies of each other, with some speculation that Thor was afraid of Jörmungandr and vice-versa. There is some amount of decoration to killing such a massive beast, perhaps a trophy in claiming his scales or fangs. However, Jörmungandr did not necessarily do anything evil. It is true that he would end up killing Thor, a beloved god, but it is his allegiance to his father in the days of Ragnarok that spurs him on rather than his hatred for Thor. The latter of the two was likely formed by fear after the fishing incident. Thor, likewise, may have hated the snake for escaping during the same incident when he could have taken its life then and ended it.

Sleipnir, the Eight Legged

Once, when a giant known only as "the builder" came to Asgard to help fortify the walls surrounding it, he brought along a stallion suited for his size named Svaldifari, who helped carry the materials. He told the Aesir that if he could finish these fortifications in three-season's time, he would take Freya, the sun, and the moon, all to himself as compensation. The gods came together in counsel and agreed that this demand was too unreasonable. Loki made the suggestion that the giant would only have a single winter to complete it, or else he would not be paid his demands. The gods, agreeing with Loki, brought their proposal to the giant who agreed to their terms so long as he was safe while working in Asgard.

To their shock, the giant's work was remarkably efficient. He was nearly complete with three days left of winter to spare. Furious, the gods turned to Loki and berated him, saying it was his fault for making the suggestion at all. They had sworn an oath to give the builder the compensation he requested, and so if he did manage to complete the project, they would have no choice but to honor his request. Loki begged their pardon and swore he would ensure this would not come to pass.

Observing the giant work, it was clear he needed his horse Svaldifari in order to bring the necessary materials and finish off the gates of the fortified walls. Seeing this, Loki transformed into a beautiful mare, causing the beast to stray from his master's side to follow him as he galloped through the trees. Svaldifari catches and ends up breeding with Loki, who most certainly had not expected this outcome. This impregnated the god of mischief, and he would become mother to the fastest horse in all the legends, Sleipnir, an eight-legged grey stallion.

The builder, for his inability to complete the task, was killed by Thor. Odin was apparently not completely appalled by Loki's exploits and took Sleipnir as his own steed. The horse was incredibly fast and powerful, in some places being considered Lord of the horses. The name Sleipnir translates, in a very fitting way when considering his speed, to "slippery."

Hraesvelgr, the Corpse-Swallower

A beautiful and terrifying creature, Hraesvelgr is a giant that takes the form of an eagle and sits upon two pillars in the realm of Hel. According to a translation of the *Poetic Edda*, Hraesvelgr is the originator of the wind itself that arises the moment the giant begins to flap his massive wings. It blows over the world of Hel, possibly being the reason why it is covered in frost and ice. He aids the goddess there who watches over the dead by observing all those who come to the land. Hraesvelgr's name translates to "Corpse-Swallower," a term which is appropriate for a giant eagle that watches over the souls of the dead.

Fenrir, the Lord of Wolves

Another of Loki's offspring, Fenrir the wolf, was raised among the Aesir in hopes they would be able to control and make use of his abilities for their own means. As he grew quickly, he became more and more wild. In the tale "The Binding of Fenrir," the gods—failing to chain him—called upon the dwarves to craft unbreakable bonds that might contain the beast. They succeed, however Fenrir bites off Tyr's hand in the process. Enraged that he would be tricked into being chained, Fenrir's saliva froths from his mouth and forms the River of Expectation. He vows to devour everything in his path when he frees himself of his bonds.

Fenrir's oath proves its validity when, during Ragnarok, he is freed of his bindings and devours the All-Father himself. Vidar, enraged, slays the enormous, malevolent wolf, thus putting to rest the very end of the world. The name Fenrir means "he who dwells in the marshes."

Skoll and Hati

Old Norse	Translation
Sköll heitir ulfr, er fylgir inu skírleita goði til varna viðar, en annarr Hati, hann er Hróðvitnir sonr, sá skal fyr heiða brúði himins.	Skoll is the name of the wolf, Who follows the shining priest Into the desolate forest, And the other is Hati, Hróðvitnir's son, Who chases the bright bride of the sky.

    McCoy translates one of the *Poetic Edda*'s poems, Grímnismál, stanza 39. He notes that the nouns priest and bride are used as male and female respectively. However, Mani is the moon and considered male, while Sol is the sun and considered female, making it unclear which exactly each wolf is chasing.

The one who mocks, Skoll, and the one who hates, Hati, are two wolves that endlessly chase after the sun and moon in the sky, attempting to devour them. They are said to be Fenrir's children, and are successful in their mission to eat the sun and moon during Ragnarok, casting the world into an endless darkness.

Trolls

Not to be confused with our modern understanding of an internet troll, these creatures are related in some way to the jötunn and are usually used in folklore to scare children into behaving. They are large creatures that sometimes roam Midgard and have been known to devour human flesh—especially of naughty children. Generally, these massive, ugly fiends can be found dwelling in mountains, caves, or anywhere dark where they can retreat from the offensive sunlight, which is said to petrify them into stone. In the Ullensvang Municipality in Vestland County, Norway, there is a popular rock formation known as Trolltunga. A large, horizontal cliff that juts out from the rocks above Ringedalsvatnet lake, it is considered to be the tongue of a petrified troll and is an extremely popular hiking destination.

Draugr

To modern audiences, the concept of a Draugr somewhat matches a typical zombie—especially with the translation of their title being *walking dead* or *ghost*—with some very notable differences. The corpses of the dead rise with knowledge of battle, usually dwelling in burial mounds full of treasure. Aside from this, they are considered among the same ranks of living pests and are generally treated as such. While they can be harmful, there is one way to end their undead wanderings; by decapitating the Draugr, placing its head on its rump, and ensuring the whole body is cremated to ashes.

Mara

A ghastly female creature said to sit on the bodies of humans and beasts as they sleep, bringing them nightmares. She may appear to be ugly or beautiful, animal or human, but she always brings ill dreams to those she visits. Some legends say humans transform into her while sleeping, blaming their lethargy on this concept altogether. This is also used to explain sleepwalking, or more often sleep *riding* on creatures like horses in the mythology.

Fossegrimen

A water spirit that plays the fiddle while floating along a stream. He often takes the form of a handsome nude man with long hair, sometimes with a lily pad on his head, resting beneath a waterfall. He minds his own business, only interacting with others after they have asked something of him. His music is enchanting, moving the hearts of all that hear it. In exchange for payment in food, he will teach any who ask how to play the fiddle. However, if bad music is played near him, his form changes into that of a terrifying monster.

Dragons

Often featured on the figureheads of Viking ships, these creatures occasionally make an appearance in Norse mythology. They are not the usual foes of the gods, however, as mortal men take up fights against them more than anything. The Midgard Serpent is considered in some respects to be a dragon that Thor fights, as there are some mentions of them both flying and crawling on land. Otherwise, they are not prominently seen often in Norse folklore.

Chapter Six: Popular Tales of the Mythology

There were countless stories told by word of mouth in Norse mythology, most of them of gods defeating warriors or giants, but some of humorous ends as well. The humans who created the lore, after all, did not always seek out legends to inspire, but also tragedies and comedies, just as we seek many genres in our modern world. These stories were the very pillars of religion and society, the centerpiece of everything the "Heathen Pagans" of old held dear.

Stories shared around the hearth at night, among companions of old when no children were near, by a minstrel singing praises, or religious officials holding their version of sermons, those stories have rich wells of culture behind them and should be respected as pinnacles of a very old belief system that predates Christianity. Here are just a few stories retold with an element of what it may have been like to hear them in the world of the Old Norse.

The Kidnapping of Idun
On a long journey in the All-Father's search for wisdom, Odin, Loki, and Hoenir find themselves as travel companions, coming to a stop for the evening. They hunt down and kill an ox, which would become their dinner. As the men huddle around the fire, eagerly awaiting their meat to cook, it is with much dismay they realize it will not brown no matter

how much heat is applied. An eagle calls out to them from a nearby tree.

"Your meat will not cook, for I have cast a spell on it," he says to them. "If you give me a share of your spoils, I will agree to remove the spell so we may all eat together."

Hungry, the men quickly agree, and the spell is lifted, allowing them to finish cooking. As it finishes, the eagle descends, taking the best, largest portion of their meal. Blinded by his hunger, Loki is immediately irritated at this display.

"Begone!" he says, thrusting a staff at the creature. "You dare to overstep the boundaries you have already violated?!" At this, the eagle drops the meat and instead takes the staff that Loki holds and lifts them both into the air. To the distress of the god, he is thrown against rocks and trees, injuring himself on the impact. The eagle laughs at his anguish. "Stop, I beg of you, stop this at once," cried Loki, clinging to the staff for dear life, afraid of falling to his death from the heights the eagle had brought him.

"You fool!" laughed the eagle. "I will put you down if you swear to me by oath that you will bring me the lovely demi-goddess Idun and all of her fruits of youth. Then, and only then, will I release you."

"I swear to you, I will do as you ask. Please, oh, please release me," begged Loki. Satisfied, the eagle safely drops him back to the ground.

Loki, bound by his oath, had no choice but to do as he had asked. Arriving back home after their journey, Loki approached Idun in her orchard.

"Idun," Loki called to her. "On my journey, I discovered a place with fruit that is sweeter and more potent than yours. The youth restored to me when I ate. it was unlike anything I had ever experienced!"

"That's marvelous," she replied, awestruck. "I didn't think it was possible to create fruits like mine at all. You must show me where you found them!"

"They are just beyond the walls of our very own Asgard," he grins, eyes gleaming with mischief. "Bring every fruit in your orchard, and we shall walk together to this secret place I have found." Agreeing to go with him, Idun filled her satchel with every fruit in her orchard so that none remained. The two hurried outside into the woods just on the outside of Asgard's walls.

"But there is nothing here," Idun says, turning to Loki in confusion. It is then that the giant Thjazi emerges from the shadows, snatching up the beautiful Idun in his hands.

"You have fulfilled your oath to me," Thjazi rumbles as he clutches the frightened Idun in one fist. "Farewell!" With a sway of his hand, Thjazi takes the form of the eagle that he had disguised himself as before, revealing the true nature of his own trickery. Clutching the screaming demi-goddess in his talons, he takes flight back to his home situated in icy towers on the highest mountain peaks of Jotunheim.

Word quickly spreads of Idun's disappearance, and it does not take long for the gods to begin to feel the effects of the lack of Idun's fruits. Graying and ageing rapidly, Odin and Hoenir go to Loki.

"Speak the truth," barks Odin. "You made your oath with that eagle, but what then? Where has Idun gone?!"

"I am afraid to say," admits the cowardly Loki. "You will probably get angry."

"He is already angry," speaks the feeble Hoenir, "and he plans to torture you unless you tell us the truth." Afraid of Odin's wrath, Loki reveals what had been a secret to him as well—the eagle that had tormented him before was none other than a giant that had spirited away the lovely Idun. Enraged, Odin sends the god of mischief to fetch her back. From her place beside Odin, Freya steps forward.

"Take my feathered cloak," the goddess says softly. "It will transform you into a falcon so that you may get there faster. Our lives depend on it, Loki." Taking the cloak, Loki set off immediately, flying through the roots of Yggdrasil to the tower of ice Thjazi called home.

It didn't take him long, and as a falcon, he dove through the windows to where Idun sat in a cage.

"Idun, it is I!" Loki cried as he took off the cloak before her.

"Thjazi has gone out, we must hurry while he is away," Idun shouts, terrified. "The Aesir will not last long without my fruits of youth!"

"I cannot free you as you are," said Loki, frantically searching for keys to unlock her. "And I won't be able to carry you home like this. I do not know what it is that I should do."

"Change me into something small, that I may escape this cage, and you can carry me home." At this suggestion, Loki gave her words some thought. Using his powers, he changed the demi-goddess into a small nut, which he slipped out of the bars. He changed back into a falcon and picked up Idun's tiny shape in his talons. Just as he was about to fly back out the window, Thjazi came through the door of his home. The giant sees the empty cage and immediately spots the transformed Loki.

"You lying fiend! Give me back my Idun," screamed Thjazi. Loki fled as fast as he could, and the tower of ice erupted, emerging from it the transformed Thjazi who was back into the shape of an eagle. Fear filled Loki's heart as he swept his wings along the branches of Yggdrasil, back to Asgard with Thjazi hot on his tail feathers.

"Gods of the Aesir, help us," Loki called as he approached the walls, dodging every attack the massive eagle swooped upon him, narrowly missing him every time. Freya looked to the skies, watching Loki fight for his and Idun's lives.

"They have returned," Freya announces to the Aesir. "Use the wood shavings from our constructions to light a blaze." The Aesir wasted no time. They gathered all that they could and set a pile just outside the walls of Asgard aflame. "Loki! Come here!"

Loki dove, passing safely through the fire without injury but setting the cloak ablaze. He tumbled to the ground in his human form, huddling around the tiny Idun in her nut form. A great roar speared throughout Asgard as Thjazi fell into the fires. He thrashed his mighty wings, sending gusts of wind that only made the fires burn hotter.

"Liars! All the gods are liars!" Thjazi screamed, his eagle-shriek piercing the ears of all.

"Then I will tell you the truth," the god Thor said, stepping forward with Mjöllnir. "You will not harm anyone else among us ever again." With that, he brought his hammer down with a resounding *crack* upon the giant's head. At last, the giant lay dead, smoldering in the fire the gods had made. Other Aesir gods huddled around Loki, ignoring his wounds.

"Where is she?! Where is Idun?" they demanded. Rasping, Loki unfurled his hands clutching the nut tightly. With a sparkle of magic, Idun in all of her beauty stepped free.

"I have been saved," Idun said. "I will go to my orchard and make new fruits for all to replenish their youth. I must hurry." She ran her small legs through the crowd, only pausing as she came to a corner. Idun looked back at the battered, tired Loki and graced him with a smile of forgiveness. "Rest, God of Mischief. You have redeemed yourself today." With that, she was away. Loki dusted himself off and passed the cloak back to Freya.

"Thank you, Freya," he murmured, hanging his head.

"Perhaps this will teach you," Freya chuckled, "not to swear your oaths to strange birds of prey."

Thor the Bride

One day when rousing himself from his slumber, Thor turned over on his side and reached for Mjöllnir, as the god never goes anywhere without it. However, as he fumbled at his bedside for his trusted hammer, he found it misplaced. *Odd*, he thinks as he turns to his slumbering wife, Sif. "My beloved," he murmurs, one large hand resting on her dainty shoulder. "Did you set my hammer aside to polish it?"

"I don't toy with your hammer," Sif yawned, rubbing sleep from her eyes. "It is not where you left it?"

"It's not . . ." Thor replied, growing increasingly worried. He got up, buckling his armor into place to search his home frantically. "It's not here!" he shouted, becoming agitated. "Where is my hammer?!"

"Look what I have found, my love," Sif calls to him, walking forward to show him a letter covered in runes. He took the letter carefully in his massive hands, reading it.

I have your hammer. Come alone to my hall in Jotunheim, and I will negotiate with you my terms to return what is yours.

Signed,

The Giant Chieftain, Thrym.

Enraged, Thor threw down the note. "Blasted giants," he howled, clenching his fists. "How dare they take what is mine! How could this have happened?!"

"Calm yourself," Sif quietly hummed, unfurling his fist delicately. "First, we should think of how to proceed. Without your hammer, you are at a disadvantage." Thor grunted as his wife did her best to keep him calm.

"I'm in no state for this negotiation Thyrm wishes to hold. I will ask Loki to go in my stead. He will find some way through this problem."

As agreed, Loki went ahead once more to the land of the giants. He approached the leader, hands clasped behind his back.

"Thyrm," He began, speaking formally. "I have arrived to negotiate with you. What will it take for you to return Mjöllnir?"

"Thor!" rumbled the giant, leaning down and squinting at the tiny figure before him. "You are so much smaller than I remember! You've grown thinner." At this, Loki did not correct him, merely smirking and raising a brow. "My eyesight has gotten poorer, but I know it is you," Thyrm continued confidently, stroking his beard. "If you want your beloved hammer back, then you must give to me the most beautiful goddess in your land, Freya. If she becomes my bride, you will have your little trinket back."

Upon Loki's return to the Aesir, a council was held with all gathered present. Loki laid out the terms, remarking upon how funny it was that he had been mistaken for Thor.

"I will not even consider this," screamed Freya at the idea of marrying the giant. "There must be another way."

"I have a suggestion," the Bifrost guardian, Heimdall, snorted. "If this Thyrm is as short-sighted as they say, perhaps Thor should present *himself* to be Freya." All present laughed at such a ridiculous suggestion, but a familiar glimmer of mischief illuminated Loki's eyes.

"Let's do it," Loki declared with a big grin.

"Absolutely not," grumbled the grumpy god of thunder, crossing his arms.

"Do you want your hammer back or not?" Loki prodded, barely containing his glee. He turned to all the Aesir present, asking them, "Is this not the best solution?" To Thor's horror, all agreed it would be done. Despite any further protest from Thor, all the goddesses and Loki gathered around him, sparing no detail in dressing the bulky god as the bride he was meant to be. Jewels of the finest quality, a necklace of Brisings around his neck, and women's clothes with a dainty veil to hide his face decorated the humiliated god, who found this all to be quite emasculating. "One last detail," Loki laughed, turning himself into a maid-servant to accompany Thor.

"Is it necessary for you to be in a dress as well?" Thor asked quizzically as Loki joined him on his chariot.

"Unlike you," Loki smirked. "I rather enjoy playing at being feminine."

The two rode together to the hall of Thrym in Jotunheim. There, Thyrm eagerly greeted the two.

"Freya!" cried the short-sighted giant, who blushed at what he thought to be his rosy-cheeked bride. "How wonderful that you are here. Come, I have prepared a feast for you and all of my kin." He took the two disguised gods to his banquet hall, where a dinner had been prepared in "Freya's" honor. As they walked, Thor kept silent. "You are so quiet, my beloved Freya," remarked Thyrm. "Are you well?"

"Oh, my lord, she was so excited when she heard that she was to be your wife, she shouted for joy for eight whole days. She has made herself hoarse!" explained Loki, elbowing the disgusted god of thunder in the ribs.

As they sat at the table, Thor, perhaps in his heated state, voraciously devoured eight salmon, an entire ox, all of the dainty sides prepared for the women, and barrel upon barrel of mead.

"I have never seen such an appetite in a woman," Thrym exclaimed, rather happy at this discovery of his bride.

"She was so thrilled to become your wife that she has not eaten anything since being told it would be her future." Loki waved his hand away, cleverly hiding his smirk behind the rim of his cup.

Thor's intense rage only grew deeper. He glared at Thrym, whom he hated more than any present for making this humiliating charade necessary.

"How she glares at me," Thyrm remarked, squinting. "Have I done something to offend my lady?"

"Of course not!" laughed Loki. "She's merely eager to be with you alone to *consummate* your marriage as soon as possible." Thor's eyes grew bloodshot, nearly crushing the goblet in his hand.

"In that case, we shouldn't tarry!" Thrym grinned. He called for a servant, fetching Mjöllnir from its hiding place as the three headed toward the altar. "Let us be wed on this joyous day! Please, use this hammer my dear Freya, that you might hallow blessings upon our wedding!" Overjoyed, Thyrm took Mjöllnir from the servant and passed it to his bride.

Once Thor held his hammer, he felt its familiar weight and gave a sigh of relief. "Thrym," he said. "I don't believe this is going to work out."

Confused, Thyrm stepped back—only to be attacked with a massive strike from the god of thunder crushing down onto his head. Loki took a step back, marveling at the carnage as days of rage bottled up by his brother took itself out upon his groom and the kin of Thryn. At last, standing in his bloodied wedding gown, Thor panted, holding up Mjöllnir in triumph. "Loki," called the exhausted Thor. "Let us be done with this place."

As the two mounted their chariot, they looked back on the halls of Thrym. "I'm eager to remove this damned dress," Thor grumbled.

"Don't you know that a good widow must wear black?" The ever-amused Loki smirked at his quip. Upon Thor's return, Asgard resumed being guarded by the mighty god of thunder, and the tale of Thor disguising himself as a bride would cause echoes of laughter to ring in Valhalla for centuries more.

The Binding of Loki

Loki, who causes the death of the beloved god Baldur by tricking his own brother to slaughter him, and subsequently preventing the resurrection by refusing to cry for Baldur's death, became the most hated of the gods. Everywhere he went, he found he was being ignored or chased down. Frightened for his own safety, Loki fled from Asgard, hiding in a mountain home on a high peak. Odin, however, knew where he was and sent Thor to retrieve and punish him. Living near a stream, Loki ran and changed into a salmon to escape into the stream, only to be caught by Thor. Unable to change form again, Loki was brought to a cave before the Aesir gods where he was pierced by three sharp rocks to bind him on his side to the ground. In his howls of agony, Odin stepped forward.

"You have taken from us, now we will take from you," Odin said, gravely. He presented his prisoners, Loki's children, Nari and Vali, and his wife, Sigyn.

"Leave them out of this!" cried the tortured Loki. "I am the one who has damned Baldur, let me suffer alone!"

"An eye for an eye," muttered the one-eyed Odin. Odin reached out his hand, placing it on the shoulder of Vali. Vali's body convulsed, then turned into that of a massive, ravenous wolf. The Aesir, Sigyn, and Loki watched in rapt horror as Vali, unable to stop his beastly urges, turned and tore his brother Nari to shreds. Nari's screams echoed in the cavern, only matched by the anguish of Loki's howls. At last, the carnage stopped. The Aesir took the entrails of Nari and wrapped them around the sobbing Loki before they turned to iron. As a final step, a poisonous snake was hung over his head so the venom would drip down and burn his face.

In that lonely place, only Sigyn remained. She stayed by her sobbing husband's side, catching the venom in a bowl before it could hurt him. She only left to empty it when it became too full; the agony of the poison hitting Loki's face caused earthquakes from his tremors of pain.

The End, The Beginning: Ragnarok

In his eternal quest for wisdom, the prophecy of the great resetting of the world came to the All-Father. There would come a winter that would last three seasons with no break for summer. Famine would spread like a plague, causing hardship and farmers to devour every last creature they had in Midgard. Tensions rose that would turn families on each other and break out into a war that stretched across the entire realm. Skoll and Hati succeed in their quest and devour the sun and moon whole to cast the realms into complete darkness. Yggdrisil's roots rumbled, crashing a massive earthquake that would loosen Fenrir from his formerly unbreakable bindings. Tsunamis caused by the shifting of Jörmungandr in response to these earthquakes took the lives of many Vikings on their ships and the mortals that made the shores their home, his venom polluting the water in his agitation. Amid this chaos, Loki's bindings also broke. His anger, hurt, and revulsion at his punishment made him see only one possible solution: destroying all who had hurt him. So, he set out to destroy the Aesir and all they represented. He went to his daughter, Hel, and told her of his plight. Enraged, the queen of the Underworld gave him an army of Draugr to wage war with. A dragon that had been gnawing at Yggdrasil's roots snapped through, releasing the fire giants of Muspelheim into the land with their leader, Surt the Black, and the frost giants that laid ready in Jotunheim, led by Hyrum. Heimdall, watching this all from his station atop the Bifrost Bridge, blew Gjallarhorn to signal that Ragnarok had begun.

Loki led his gathered forces of chaos against the forces of order, led by Odin himself. War was unleashed, battles fought between the Aesir, the giants, and monsters galore who filled Midgard. The warriors of Valhalla came from their golden gates, winged Valkyries joined to crush the rotting skulls of Draugr in their hands. The Muspelheim giants broke the Bifrost Bridge, severing the connections to the rest of the reinforcements the Aesir may have had. In a final moment of silence before battle begins, Odin speaks to his friend, the severed head of Mimir.

"My friend," Odin speaks softly in his throne room when alone with the head. "Soothe my anxiety. Tell me, all will be well."

"My wisdom is limited here, All-Father," Mimir replies sadly. "But I know I will remember our time with fondness, and that our time here, as the Aesir gods, will be known by all."

Odin went to the battle. Odin falls, eaten by Loki's son; Fenrir is then slain by Vidar; Freya/Frigg and Freyr are cut down by Surt; Thor and Jörmungandr, another son of Loki, battle to the death; Tyr and the guardian of Hel, a wolf named Garm, end each other. Then at long last, Loki faces down with Heimdall.

"You fool," Heimdall mutters as he stands before Loki, his weapon drawn. "You're killing us all. Your children fall at your feet, the fate of man is being destroyed, are you yet satisfied?"

"I am satisfied," replies Loki, rage in his eyes. "If I can destroy this forsaken world, if I can dismantle it with the chaos I have created and put an end to this "order" that you all hold dear, then no matter the cost I will have my revenge."

The two began a battle that looked like a wild dance, harming each other with their blows, until at last, they both fell. Both cutting each other down simultaneously, there was no victor in their fight. Surt cut the ground with his flaming sword, leaving the entire world in nothing but ashes and embers that consumed Asgard. Oceans rose, drowning all those that remained. Destruction ruled all.

    Much later, as the oceans receded and the fires ate their last meal, Yggdrasil fell apart. Inside, two mortals, a man and a woman remained. Hidden there by the Aesir, the mortals named Lif and Lifthrasir's love would repopulate the earth. The Kingdom of Asgard no more, in its place rose a land of peace. Six gods remained. Two survivors of Ragnarok, Vidar and Vali, the two sons of Thor, Magni and Modi, who took up their father's hammer, and two familiar faces who emerge from the land of the unguarded Hel, the twins Baldur and Hodr. The six reconvene, vowing to learn from the mistakes of those that came before them, and promising that the new world they have inherited shall never meet the fate of the old one.

Chapter Seven: Norse Mythology in Modern Media

In the age of the Vikings, the Norse gods were worshipped in ways that, at the time, seemed fitting to the station of gods. The sacrificing of animals during festivals or holding the festivals in the honor of the gods on certain days was not unheard of in this era. These days, rather than shouting prayers in the forms of poems to the skies, those that currently practice this religion have a much less bloody way of making their offerings. In general, the mass audience that knows about Norse mythology is not learning from ancient writings, runes on rocks, or songs of praise, but rather through the tributes paid to them in the entertainment industry.

Norse Mythology in Movies and Television

Unless you are someone that doesn't care for movies and TV, it would be difficult not to know about the Marvel Cinematic Universe. Their titular movie with the title character "Thor" (2011) has several sequels that then contribute into dozens of films featuring the character of the same name from Norse mythology right alongside his brother, Loki. In these movies, Thor fights frost giants, his brother, and against Ragnarok itself, only to then fight *alongside* Marvel's titular characters like Iron Man and Captain America. Tonally, the concept of Thor as a character stays quite close to how he's originally portrayed in the world of myths, simply modernized to be understood by an audience in this era. The humanity of the gods was what was important to those that worshipped them before, a trait that actor Chris Hemsworth portrays well while playing the character. In this film franchise, Thor appears alongside Odin, Heimdall, and many others from Norse mythology set among the nine realms, including Asgard.

However, from the popularity of the "Thor" franchise came another with it, named "Loki" that debuted in May 2021. A TV series created by Disney, Tom Hiddleston returns to his role as the title character after playing him in the original "Thor" lineup. This is due to the popularity of the character, who has become notoriously infamous among fans for his charming, fun, and anti-hero type personality. Ironic that a god who was once created to be hated is now considerably one of the most beloved gods in the entire pantheon.

There are also many other interpretations and stories in the cinematic medium spread around the world, having come from inspirations of the original legends. The television series "Vikings" (2013) depicts what life was like in the Viking age, while a New Zealand production called "The Almighty Johnsons" (2011) attempted to bring humor to the concept of reincarnated gods in the modern world. The use of the pantheon can be found in several other pieces of cinematic media if one only takes a moment to seek it out.

Norse Mythology in Video Games

In recent years, several video games have made use of Norse mythology to create a fun, Viking atmosphere for players to enjoy on their own. Marco Vito Oddo of collider.com explains the appeal, "There's something about Norse mythology games that keep bringing gamers back. While everyone is kind of a dick in Greek mythology, Norse mythology is all about honor and holding the line with your brothers to face enormous challenges. Norse myths also revolve around the glory of never giving up and fighting until the very end. It's no wonder so many people are attracted to the Viking life." Among the list this quote comes from, Oddo goes on to point out a few games where gamers are getting their Viking thrill: "Assassin's Creed Valhalla" (2020). "Valheim" (2021). "God of War" (2018). "Hellblade: Senua's Sacrifice" (2017). These games are sure to offer an experience that will please anyone wanting to become a Viking themselves.

Norse Mythology in Music

Viking metal is a subgenre of black metal characterized by its chaotic and noisy sound, slow pace, use of keyboards, dark and violent imagery, and, primarily, lyrical themes of Norse mythology, Norse paganism, and the Viking Age. It is inspired by classical, operatic music, and folk metal genres with some notable contributors being the artists Mithotyn and Falkenbach.

Norse Mythology in Books

The legends of the gods are not always present in the name of the books, but the concept of the culture and the magic within these legends are in several novels of different varieties and genres. Fantasy novels about faeries have incorporated Valhalla, and this same use of Valhalla appears in several other places. Notably, as the Marvel Cinematic Universe stems from the comics that hold the same name, it is the root of these comics that sprouted into the arching narrative of the cinematic world.

Final Words

When examining the rich tales of the Norse, it isn't hard to see why they are so popular in the modern day or why they inspire so many stories even now. The human aspects of what it means to be a god are not uncharacteristic to many other religions formed around this time, and the concept of a god being perfect did not exist until Christianity became so prevalent over the time of the crusades. Vikings prayed to people who were so imperfect that they caused their own doom. Was Loki meant to be looked upon with sympathy or disdain? Was he a story that, collectively, was meant as a warning, or was he merely a creature no one wanted?

It is human to want to look up to other humans, which may be why there are so many anti-heroes and villains common among these legends. This book has merely been a taste of what Norse mythology has to offer and looking into it further is not only ideal but encouraged.

www.ingramcontent.com/pod-product-compliance
Lightning Source LLC
LaVergne TN
LVHW021735060526
838200LV00052B/3297